10/19

Failure to return
Library Material
is a crime —
N.C. General
Statutes # 14-398

Pender County Public Library
Hampstead Branch
Hampstead, NC 28443

PLEASE JOIN
MOVE IT!

Caroline Alliston

Quarto is the authority on a wide range of topics.
Quarto educates, entertains and enriches the lives of our readers—enthusiasts and lovers of hands-on living.
www.quartoknows.com

Developed and written by: Caroline Alliston MA(Cantab), MSc, CEng FIMechE
Illustrator: Tom Connell
Photograper: Michael Wicks
Model maker: Fiona Hayes
Consultants: John Harvey BEng, CEng MIMechE,
Dr. Alex Alliston MA(Cantab), CEng MIMechE
Design and editorial: Starry Dog Books Ltd

© 2019 Quarto Publishing plc

This library edition published in 2019 by Quarto Library,
an imprint of The Quarto Group.
6 Orchard Road, Suite 100
Lake Forest, CA 92630
T: +1 949 380 7510
F: +1 949 380 7575
www.QuartoKnows.com

All rights reserved. No part of this publication may be reproduced, stored in a retrieval system, or transmitted in any form or by any means (including electronic, mechanical, photocopying, recording, or otherwise) without prior written permission from the publisher.

ISBN 978-0-7112-4220-3

Manufactured in Dongguan, China TL012019

9 8 7 6 5 4 3 2 1

INTERNET SAFETY

Children should be supervised when using the internet, particularly when using an unfamiliar website for the first time. Publisher and author cannot be held responsible for the content of the websites referred to in this book.

CONTENTS

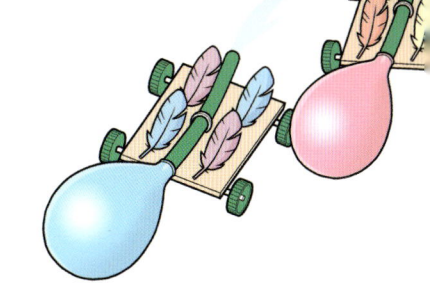

BE INSPIRED! ----------------------- 5

CARTESIAN DIVER ---------------- 6

SAILBOAT ---------------------------- 8

BALLOON BUGGY ------------------10

MARBLE RUN -----------------------14

COLORED SPINNER ---------------18

MARBLE MAZE -------------------- 22

ORBITING IN SPACE -------------- 24

GLOSSARY AND
FIND OUT MORE ------------------ 30

INDEX ---------------------------------- 32

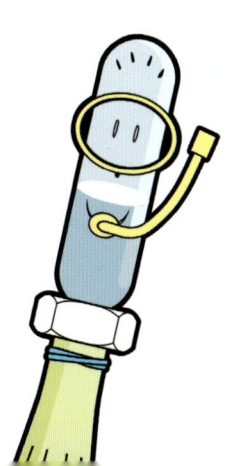

FOREWORD

Be inspired to make our world a better place.

We live in a "made" world. Without the advances made by engineers and scientists, we simply would not have the houses, cars, food, clothes, health care, and entertainment that we enjoy. Today we face truly global challenges, such as feeding a growing population and combating climate change.

This book provides seven exciting and engaging projects to encourage creative thinking and problem solving. I hope it will inspire future generations of engineers and scientists that are needed to make our world a better place.

Dr. Colin Brown CEng FIMechE, FIMMM,
CEO, Institution of Mechanical Engineers

BE INSPIRED!

Test your design, creativity, and engineering skills with these seven exciting projects and challenges.

WORK SAFELY

Always get permission from an adult before beginning a project and ask for their help when necessary.

SCISSORS
Be careful not to cut yourself with scissors. If using nail scissors, don't poke yourself—ask an adult to start the cut for you.

WOODEN SKEWERS
To avoid injuries, cut about 1/4 inch off the sharp tips, leaving the sticks slightly pointed to help you assemble the models.

GLUE GUNS
Only use low melt temperature glue guns; high melt glue guns can burn you badly. Use a gluing mat to protect your table. Avoid getting glue on your clothes. Make sure your hands and gluing area are dry before you switch on a glue gun. If you don't have a glue gun, most of the models can be made using double-sided foam tape—we recommend 1/2 inch wide x 1/32 inch thick, super-sticky.

USING ELECTRICITY
Always be careful when using electricity. Make sure you operate electrical appliances correctly and safely.

JUNIOR HACKSAWS AND DRILLS
Make sure you clamp your work in the vise so that you don't cut your fingers.

SHARP PENCILS
Be careful not to poke yourself with sharp pencils, and don't put them near your eyes.

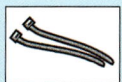
CABLE TIES
Be careful not to fasten cable ties around your fingers.

GET READY

Before you start a project, make sure you have at hand all the tools and materials that you'll need—each project has its own YOU WILL NEED list. Then read the easy-to-follow, illustrated, step-by-step instructions to find out how to make the models. Discover more in the NOW YOU CAN activities and HOW IT WORKS explanations.

Cheap, everyday, and recycled household objects are used wherever possible. Collect old CDs and DVDs, thin sheets of polystyrene foam, corks, plastic bottle caps, and plastic drink bottles of various sizes.

Wood and fasteners can be bought from home improvement stores.

TAKE CARE!

Look out for the "Take Care!" symbol, which refers you to the warning instructions on the first page of each project. Craft knives, power tools, and small pruning shears should only be used by an adult.

YOU WILL NEED:

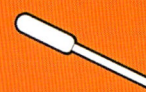

1 plastic pipette
5 ml (or 3 ml)

1 M10 nut
(M8 nut if using
3 ml pipette)

1 foam craft sheet
1/16 inch thick

1 small rubber band

1 transparent plastic
drink bottle,
easy to squeeze

FROM YOUR TOOLBOX:

- ruler • scissors
- permanent marker
- felt-tip pen

CARTESIAN DIVER

Make a diver sink to the bottom of a bottle and rise up again!

DID YOU KNOW?

"Cartesian" comes from the name Descartes. René Descartes was the 17th-century French scientist and mathematician who is said to have invented this experiment.

1 To make the diver, push the nut onto the pipette and cut to the length shown. Draw on a face with a permanent marker.

2 Draw this shape on the foam and cut it out. Wrap it around the pipette just below the nut, and hold it in place with a rubber band.

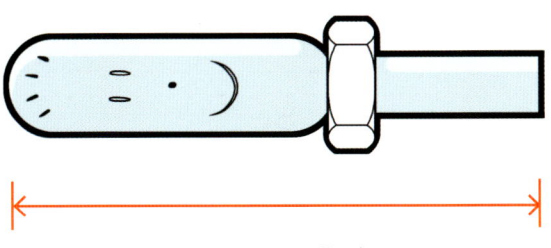

3 1/4 inches for 5 ml pipette
2 3/8 inches for 3 ml pipette

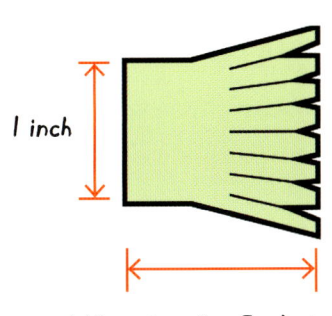

1 inch

1 1/2 inches for 5 ml pipette
1 inch for 3 ml pipette

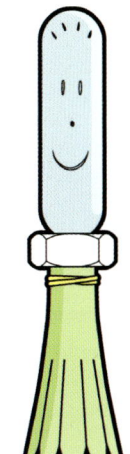

3 Fill the bottle with water, push the diver in, and screw on the lid. Squeeze the bottle to make the diver sink. Release it and the diver will rise back to the top!

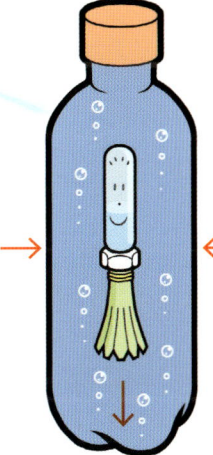

NOW YOU CAN...

* Watch the water level in the pipette rise as you squeeze the bottle and fall again when you release the bottle.

HOW IT WORKS

The diver includes both air, which is light, and a heavy metal nut. In order to float, the diver needs to be lighter than the same amount of water. When you squeeze the bottle, pressure is passed through the water, squashing (compressing) the air in the pipette. This partly fills with water, so the diver becomes heavier and sinks. When you release the bottle the air expands, pushing the water back out, and the diver becomes lighter and rises.

YOU WILL NEED:

1 large polystyrene foam disc about 3/16 inch thick x 10 inches or more in diameter

1 wooden skewer (cut off the sharp tip)

1 sheet of thin cardboard, such as the side of a cereal box

1 plastic bottle cap

optional, 1 sailor e.g. small plastic toy (or you can make your own)

FROM YOUR TOOLBOX:

- ruler • felt-tip pen • large scissors • sharp pencil
- adhesive putty • low melt glue gun • hole punch

SAILBOAT

Turn a sheet of foam into a boat to sail across your bath.

TAKE CARE with the sharp pencil.

1 Draw a boat base on your foam disc and cut it out. Make it roughly as long as the foam disc and quite wide.

2 Make a hole in the bottle cap (see page 12, step 5) and glue it on. Push the skewer (the mast) through the hole into the base.

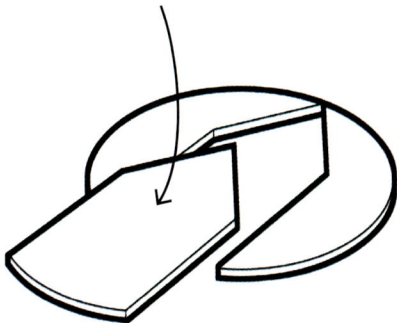

If the base is too narrow, the boat may capsize.

Put the mast toward the front so the wind in the sail pulls the boat along.

3 Make a card sail slightly shorter than the mast. Punch a hole top and bottom and slide it on. Float your boat on water and blow into the sail.

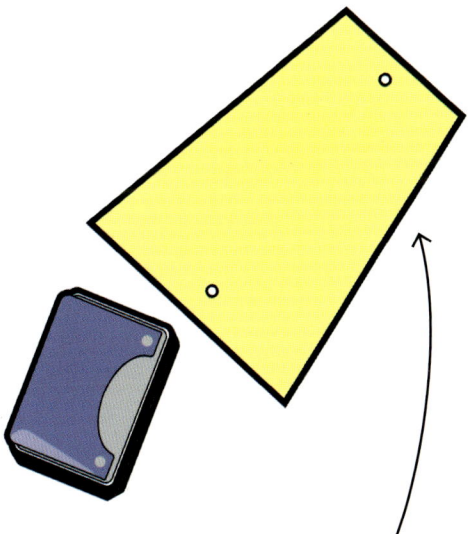

If the sail is narrower at the top, the boat is less likely to fall over when you blow it along.

HOW IT WORKS

This sailboat design, similar to that used by the ancient Egyptians, only sails in the direction the wind is blowing. Nowadays sailboats are designed to also sail across the wind.

NOW YOU CAN...

* Decorate your boat and add a sailor.

* Add a keel and use a triangular sail so your boat can sail across the wind.

YOU WILL NEED:

1 sheet of corrugated cardboard or plastic roughly 1/8 inch thick

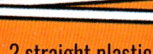

2 straight plastic drinking straws

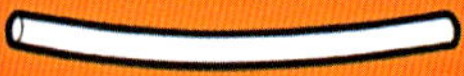

1 length of garden hose or plastic tube, about 9/16 inch diameter x 10 inches long

Cable ties/zip ties 4–8 inches long

2 wooden skewers

4 plastic bottle caps

1 round party balloon

Lightweight decorations e.g. feathers, tinsel (optional)

FROM YOUR TOOLBOX:

- sharp pencil • ruler
- large scissors • low melt glue gun or double-sided foam tape • pencil sharpener • adhesive putty
- small pruning shears

BALLOON BUGGY

Make a balloon buggy that whizzes along the ground.

⚠ **TAKE CARE** with the sharp pencil. Only adults should use the small pruning shears.

1 Draw a rectangle on your corrugated sheet as shown and cut it out. This will be the base of the buggy.

2 Draw a line across each end of the board, 1 inch in from the edges. Stick two 6-inch-long straws onto the lines.

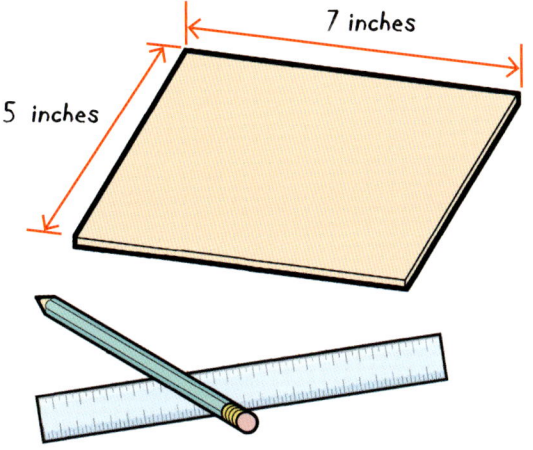

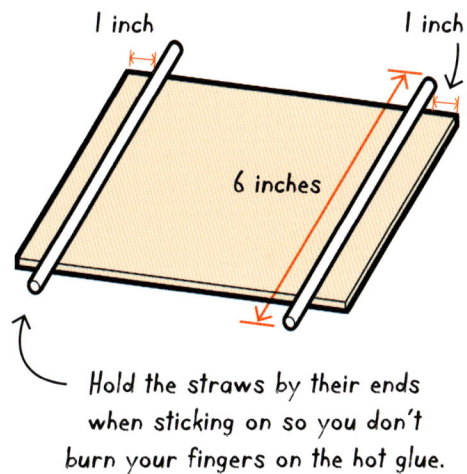

Hold the straws by their ends when sticking on so you don't burn your fingers on the hot glue.

3 Turn the base over and attach the hose. The curved ends must point upward to prevent the balloon from rubbing on the ground.

4 Use the scissors to cut off the sharp tips of the wooden skewers. Sharpen the blunt ends slightly—this will help the wheels to go on.

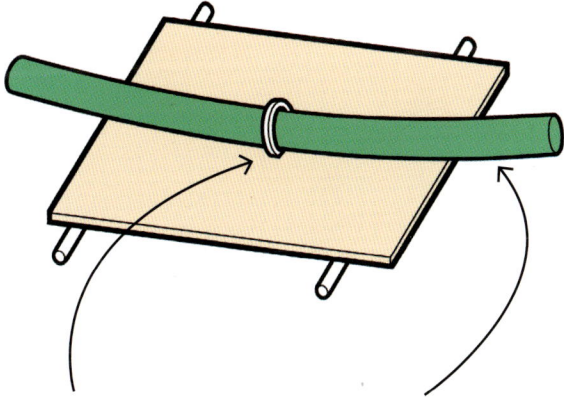

Pierce two holes in the base. Fasten the hose on firmly with a cable tie.

If the hose has curved ends, make sure they point upwards.

Just cut off the very tip so you don't poke yourself.

Push each plastic bottle cap, open end downward, onto a lump of adhesive putty. Use a sharp pencil to make a hole in the middle of each one.

 Slide the skewers (axles) through the straws. Push the lids on to the skewers until they almost touch the ends of the straws. Ask an adult to cut off the skewer ends with small pruning shears.

Don't make the hole too big—it will need to be a tight fit on the skewer.

Keep the pencil upright or the lead may snap.

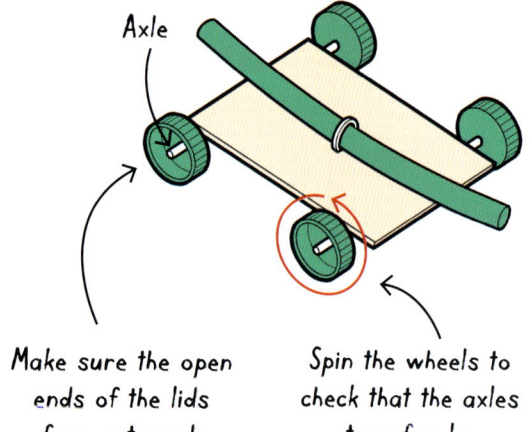

Axle

Make sure the open ends of the lids face outward.

Spin the wheels to check that the axles turn freely.

7 Slide the balloon onto the hose. Blow through the other end to inflate the balloon, squeeze the neck, place on a smooth floor, then let go.

8 You can color or paint your buggy, or add some lightweight decorations, such as feathers.

If the balloon comes off while blowing up, attach the neck to the tube with a cable tie.

Keep decorations light—extra weight will slow your buggy down!

NOW YOU CAN...

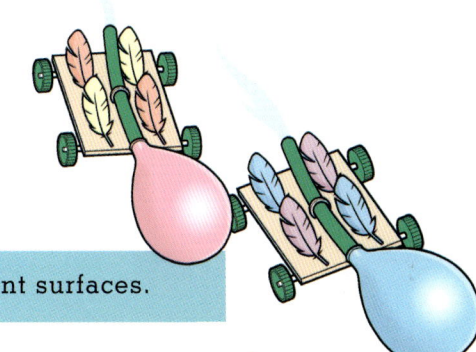

* Challenge a friend to see whose buggy travels the farthest.

* Test your buggy on different surfaces.

* Try using different tube diameters or different sizes and shapes of balloon to see which work best.

* Make changes to the buggy to stop the balloon from rubbing on the ground.

* Repair your buggy! If the straws come loose, secure them with cable ties—but don't pull the ties too tight or you'll stop the axles from rotating freely.

HOW IT WORKS

Compressed air is stored in the balloon. When you release the neck of the balloon, a jet of air is pushed out of the other end of the tube. This acts like a rocket, pushing the buggy forward. The surface the buggy is on needs to be smooth. If there's too much friction, the air jet won't be able to overcome it and the buggy won't move.

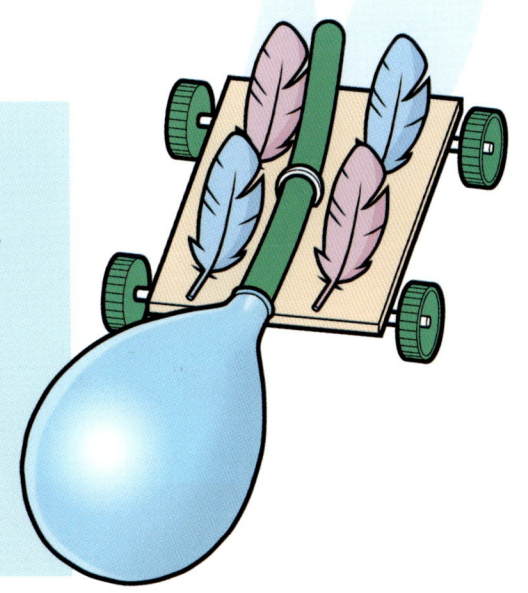

13

YOU WILL NEED:

1 board e.g. corrugated cardboard, MDF, or hardboard roughly 3/16 inch thick x 16 x 24 inches

2 strips corrugated cardboard 2 1/2 x 24 inches

2 strips corrugated cardboard 2 1/2 x 16 inches

1 marble

1 or 2 plastic drink bottles

Variety of materials such as cardboard tubes, corrugated cardboard or plastic, packaging material, etc.

FROM YOUR TOOLBOX:

- low melt glue gun • large scissors • nail scissors
- tape • sandpaper
- stopwatch

MARBLE RUN

Can your marble zigzag down the track and meet the 10-second challenge?

TAKE CARE using nail scissors—ask an adult to start the cut.

CHALLENGE

THE CHALLENGE...

1. The marble must travel from the top to the bottom of the run in as close to 10 seconds as possible.
2. Your run must be no more than 24 inches high and 16 inches wide.
3. You can take as long as you like to build your marble run.

1 Glue the four strips of corrugated cardboard to the edges of the board, as shown. These will stop the marble from falling off the sides.

2 Design and make a stand for your marble run and glue it to the back of the board.

Can you think of a way to make the stand adjustable so that you can alter the tilt and change the speed of the marble?

Glue the edges together.

The edges will help to stiffen the board if it is made of cardboard.

If the board tilts backward slightly, the marble is less likely to fall off the front.

Using nail scissors, cut the top off a plastic bottle to make a funnel. Cut away an arch shape from the top cardboard strip and glue the funnel in place.

 Make a track down the board for the marble. Try out each section before adding the next. Include lots of strips at shallow angles.

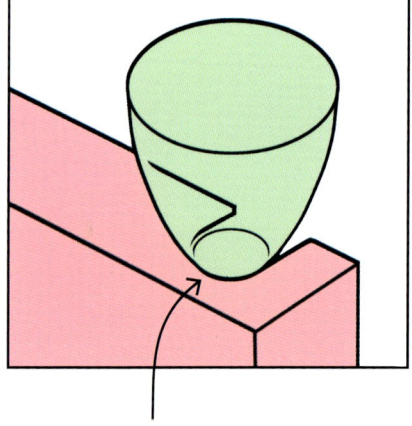

The arch shape should just fit the neck of the bottle.

Try taping a section on to test it before gluing it in place.

 Stick rough surfaces to the strips to slow the marble down. If your marble falls off, add front edges to the strips.

 Now time how long it takes for the marble to travel from the top to the bottom of your marble run.

Sandpaper *Front edge* *Cut the bottom off a plastic bottle to make a marble catcher.*

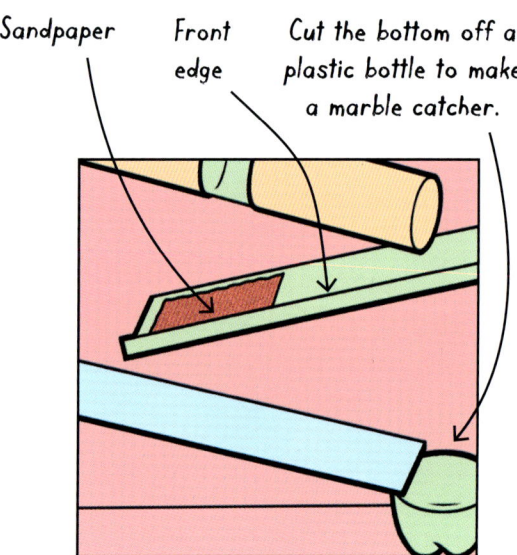

How close can you get to 10 seconds?

HOW IT WORKS

The marble is pulled downward by gravity. If allowed to fall freely, it would take only a fraction of a second to fall the height of the board. You have slowed it down by making it travel farther, stop, and change direction, and by using different slopes. Using rough or bumpy materials also slows it down.

NOW YOU CAN...

Make some changes to get even closer to the target time of 10 seconds.

* Alter the slope of some of the strips to slow down or speed up the marble.

* Modify the stand to alter the tilt of the marble run.

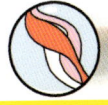

* Change the surfaces of some strips. If you've used corrugated cardboard strips, try removing some of the top surface so that the marble runs on the bumpy corrugations.

* Put in small ramps and jumps.

* Try adding a "loop the loop"!

COLORED SPINNER

Experiment with color blending by making a spinning colored disc.

YOU WILL NEED:

1 plastic tube with lid fitted roughly 1-inch inside diameter x 5 1/2 inches long

String 22 inches long

1 wooden rod 1/4-inch diameter

1 cork preferably plastic

2 old CDs or DVDs

1 sheet of cardstock about 1/16 inch thick

1 printer-size sheet of thin white cardstock

FROM YOUR TOOLBOX:

- ruler • marker • pencil
- vise • drill with 1/8"- & 15/64"- diameter drill bits
- sandpaper • large scissors
- junior hacksaw • pencil sharpener • low melt glue gun • pair of compasses
- colored felt-tip pens
- double-sided tape

TAKE CARE using the saw and drill—ask an adult for help.

1 Gently clamp the tube in the vise and drill a ¹⁵⁄₆₄" hole 1 inch from the lid end. Remove the lid and smooth around the hole with sandpaper.

2 Saw off 8 inches of rod. Saw a small notch 3 inches from one end. Saw off a separate 2-inch length to make a handle and cut a small notch in the middle.

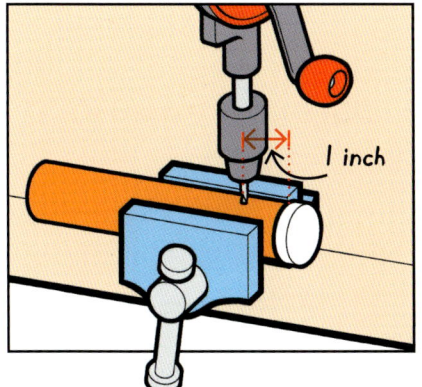

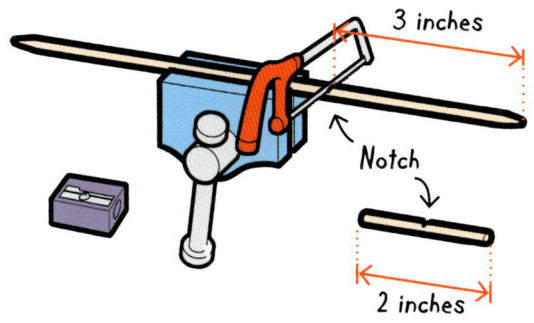

You can support the tube with wood so it doesn't move when you drill it.

Sharpen the ends of the rod slightly. Smooth both pieces with sandpaper.

3 Slide the rod into the tube, notched end first. Saw the cork in half. Drill a ⅛" pilot hole through one half, then enlarge it to ¹⁵⁄₆₄". Push the half cork onto the rod until it is ¼ inch above the rim, as shown.

4 Glue the two CDs together, then glue them to the top of the cork, lining up the hole centers. Cut a 1 ½-inch-wide disc of thick cardstock and drill a ¹⁵⁄₆₄" hole through it. Put glue on the CD inner circle and cork top, then push the cardstock disc down firmly onto the glue before it cools.

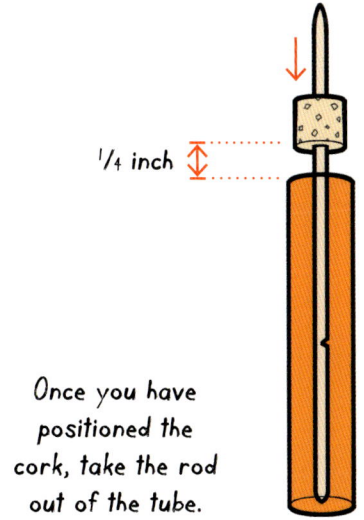

Once you have positioned the cork, take the rod out of the tube.

Before gluing, push the cardstock disc onto the rod to make sure it fits, then remove it.

Glue here.

Tie a slip knot in one end of the string and loop it over the notch in the handle. Slide the other end into the hole in the tube, as shown. Tie another slip knot and loop it over the notch in the rod.

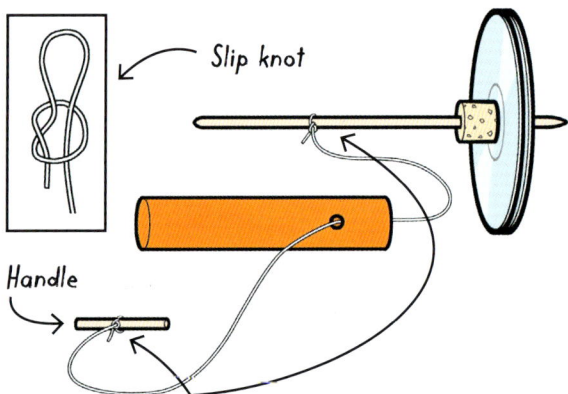

Pull the string hard to tighten the knots. Try to jam it in the notches so it can't come loose.

 Slide the rod back into the plastic tube. Pull the handle until all the loose string is hanging out. Turn the CD unit to wind in the string.

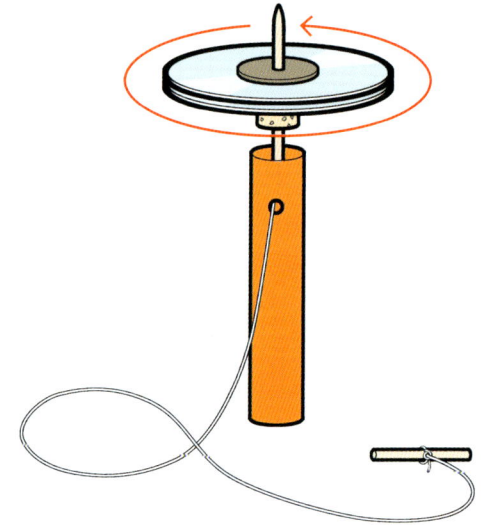

7 Hold the tube and pull the handle to spin the CD unit. Just before the string is fully out, leave it slack so it winds back in.

Pull the string again to make the unit spin the other way, then repeat.

8 Draw a 2 3/8-inch-radius disc on white cardstock. Draw three inner circles, as shown. Cut out the disc and center circle. Color the rings with repeating colors. Tape it to the top of the CD unit and spin!

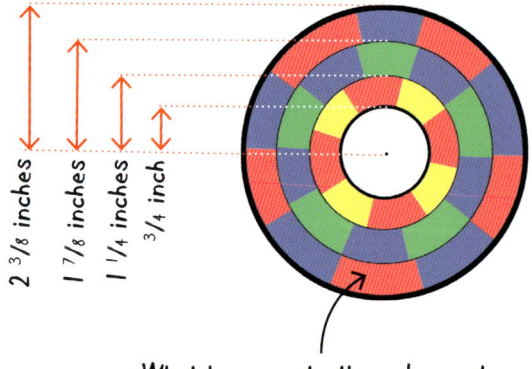

What happens to the colors when you spin the disc?

NOW YOU CAN...

* Color some more cardstock discs in different colors and try them out. It's possible to get three discs from one printer-size sheet of cardstock.

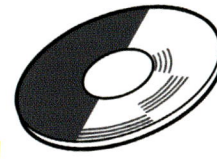
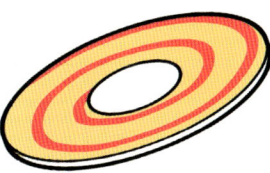

* Make a Newton disc, named after the 17th-century British scientist Sir Isaac Newton, who invented it. Color it with the colors of the rainbow. A rainbow is caused by raindrops splitting white light from the sun into its separate colors, so if you mix light from all the colors of the rainbow you should get white, or nearly white!

* Fix your spinner! If the string comes loose on the rod, tighten it back up. If your CD unit comes loose, glue it back on.

HOW IT WORKS

Pulling the string makes the CD unit spin and gives it kinetic (movement) energy. When you stop pulling, the energy in the CD unit makes it keep turning, winding the string back in again. Sharpening the bottom of the rod allows it to spin more easily. If the colored circles move fast enough, the colors appear to mix together and produce different colors. For example, red and yellow mix to make orange, and blue and red make purple. On a television screen, red, green, and blue light are mixed in different amounts to make all the other colors.

MARBLE MAZE

Design a tricky marble maze, full of false trails and dead ends.

YOU WILL NEED:

1 board e.g. MDF, hardboard or plywood roughly 1/8 inch thick x 12 inches x 12 inches

13 feet square section wood 3/8 inch or 1/2 inch square

1 marble

FROM YOUR TOOLBOX:

- sandpaper • ruler • pencil
- vise • junior hacksaw
- low melt glue gun • sheet of 11x17 inch (A3) paper

TAKE CARE using the saw—ask an adult for help.

AIM OF THE GAME...

The aim is to tilt the board and make the marble roll its way through the maze without getting stuck in the false trails.

1 Measure and cut four edge pieces. Smooth with sandpaper and glue them to the base.

If your board is rough on one side, use it smooth side up.

Vise

Junior hacksaw

2 On paper, design a maze in which the marble has to travel around most of the board.

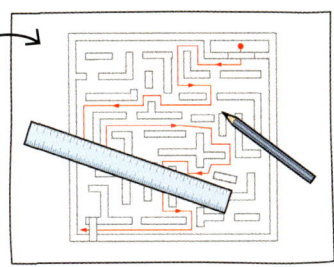

Include false trails with dead ends or gaps slightly too small for the marble.

3 Prepare each piece of wood in turn and glue it on, checking the gap size with the marble.

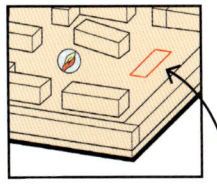

Mark the position before gluing so the piece ends up in the right place.

4 Try out the maze—check that the marble runs along the real trail but not the false trails.

HOW IT WORKS

When you tilt the board, the marble rolls downhill due to gravity—a force that pulls things toward the ground. Adjust the direction of tilt to make the marble roll around the obstacles.

NOW YOU CAN...

* Mark the start and finish with arches or labels.

* Challenge friends to see who can finish fastest.

ORBITING IN SPACE

Make a moving model of Earth orbiting the sun while the moon orbits Earth.

YOU WILL NEED:

1 wooden rod 4 inches long to fit pulley

1 base, plywood or MDF, 1/8 x 2 x 6 inches

1 pulley about 1 1/4–2-inches diameter, 1/8–1/4 inch central hole

1 piece of wood about 3/8 x 1 x 4 inches

1 rubber band 1/32 x 1/16 x 3–4 inches

3 pop rivets, 1/8" diameter x 1/4"

1 plastic tube or straw, 1/4 inch diameter x 2 3/4 inches long

1 motor pulley, tight fit on motor shaft, overall diameter 5/16 inch, pulley inner diameter 1/8 inch

1 thin plastic tube, 1/16 inch inside diameter x 2 3/8 inches

1 white bead (Moon), about 5/16 inch diameter, 1/8 inch hole

1 wooden skewer, 2 inch length

2 polystyrene balls (Earth & sun) 3/8-inch & 1 1/2-inches diameter
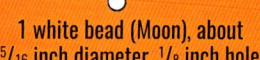

FROM YOUR TOOLBOX:

• pencil sharpener • ruler
• pencil • vise • drill, 1/8"- & 3/16"- drill bits & drill bit same diameter as rod • sandpaper
• junior hacksaw • low melt glue gun • plastic bottle cap 1-inch diameter • wood file
• paintbrush • acrylic paints

TAKE CARE using the drill and saw—ask an adult for help.

SUN UNIT

 Sharpen both rod ends slightly. Mark 5/8 inch from one end of the rod, then push on the pulley until the mark just shows.

 Drill a hole, the same diameter as the rod, through the base. Smooth the base with sandpaper. Check that the rod turns easily in the hole.

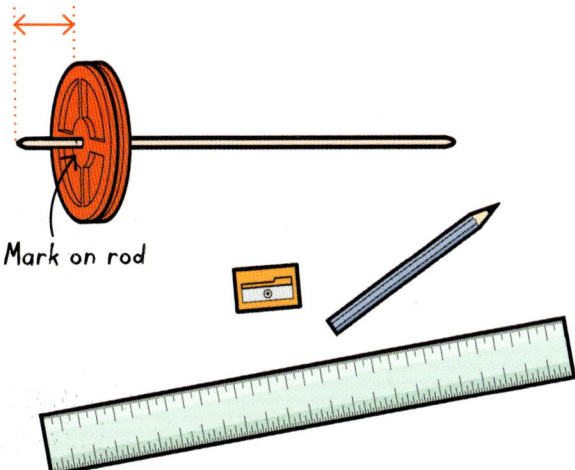

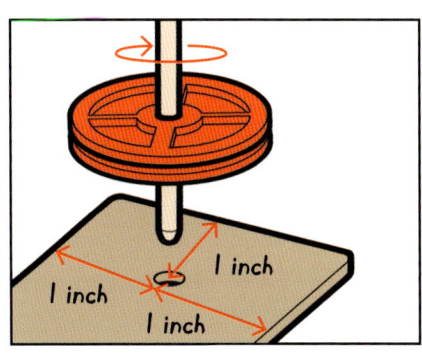

If the rod doesn't turn easily, run the drill through the hole again.

 Saw off 1 inch of wood to make a handle. Drill a hole, the same diameter as the rod, through the middle. Push the 5/8-inch rod end into the handle.

 Hold the handle with one hand and rotate the base around it with the other. The base should turn easily, while the rod and pulley stay still.

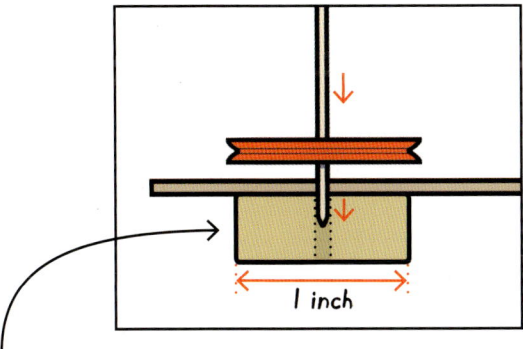

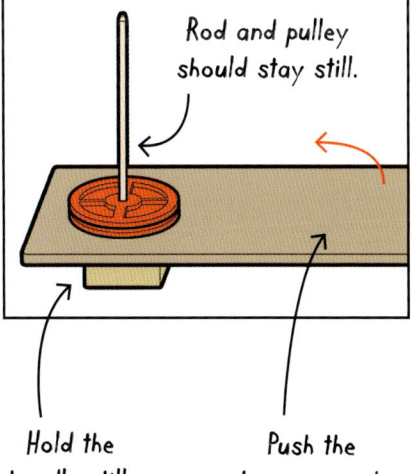

Smooth all sides and edges of the handle with sandpaper.

If either the pulley or handle is loose on the rod, glue them on, but don't glue them to the base.

Hold the handle still.

Push the base around.

 **5** Fit the rubber band over the pulley and lay it along the base. Mark a cross at the end. Remove the rubber band.

EARTH UNIT

  6 Mark a second cross $3/4$ inch farther along. At this mark, drill an $1/8"$ hole through the base to fit the first pop rivet.

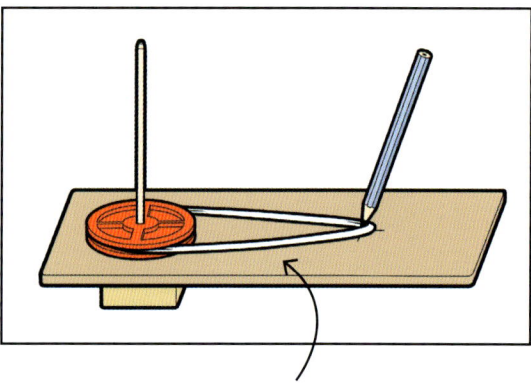

Don't stretch the rubber band.

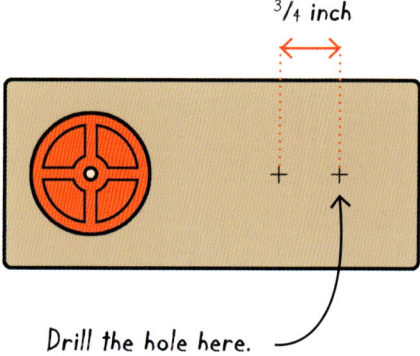

Drill the hole here.

  7 Saw off 1 inch of wood, drill an $1/8"$ hole through the middle, and smooth the edges. Push the thick end of the first pop rivet through the base into the wood.

  8 Draw around the bottle lid on the remaining wood. Saw roughly around the disc, then round it off using a file. Drill a $3/16"$ hole through the middle.

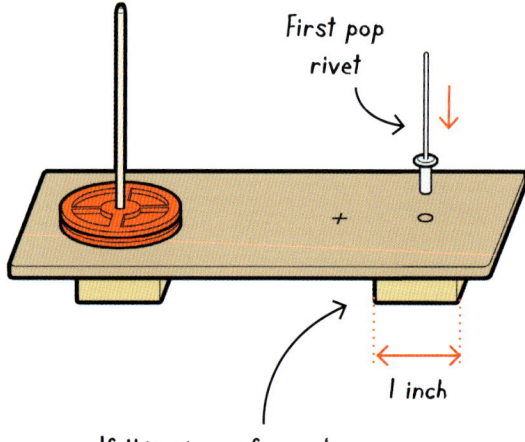

First pop rivet

If this piece of wood is loose, glue it on.

1 inch

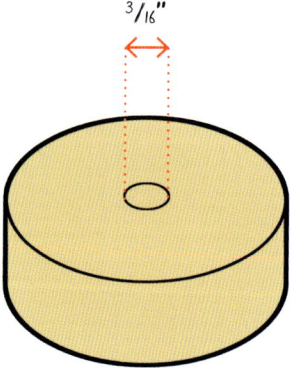

Smooth any rough edges with sandpaper.

9 Push the motor pulley into the disc from one side and push the 1/4-inch-diameter tube in from the other side.

MOON UNIT

10 ⚠️ Drill an 1/8" hole to one side of the tube, with the drill held at a slight angle. Push the thick end of the second pop rivet into the hole, as shown.

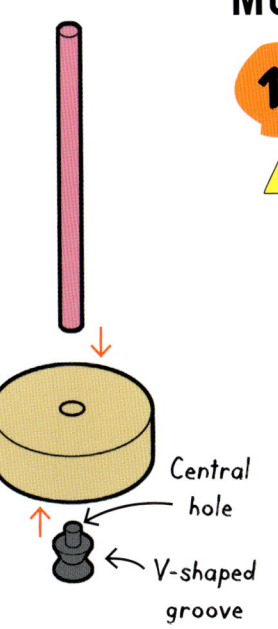

If anything is loose in its hole, glue it in, but don't get glue in the central hole or V-shaped groove of the pulley.

Central hole

V-shaped groove

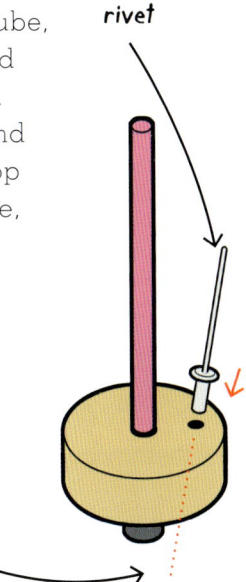

Second pop rivet

The slight angle of the hole is so the moon doesn't touch Earth.

11 Glue the moon onto the thick end of the third rivet. Join the two rivets together end to end with the thin tube, as shown.

12 Slide the motor pulley onto the thin part of the first pop rivet in the base. Spin to check that the unit rotates freely on the rivet.

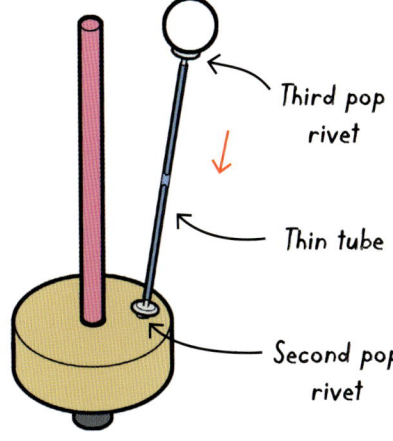

If any rivets are loose, glue them in.

Third pop rivet

Thin tube

Second pop rivet

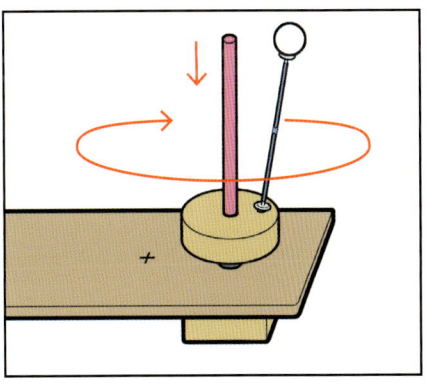

If the unit does not rotate freely, make sure there is no glue in the central hole.

27

FINISHING TOUCHES

 Push the sun onto the rod. Sharpen one end of the skewer and push it into Earth. Slide the other end into the 1/4-inch-diameter tube and glue in place.

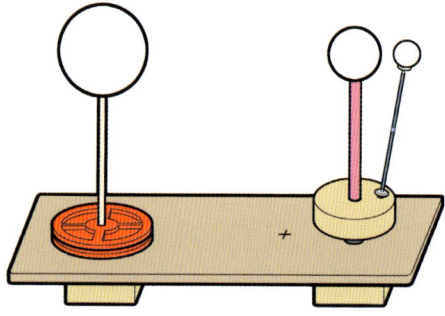

Adjust the sun, Earth, and moon to roughly the same height.

14 Lift the Earth unit off the first rivet. Place the rubber band around both pulleys and slide the unit back onto the rivet.

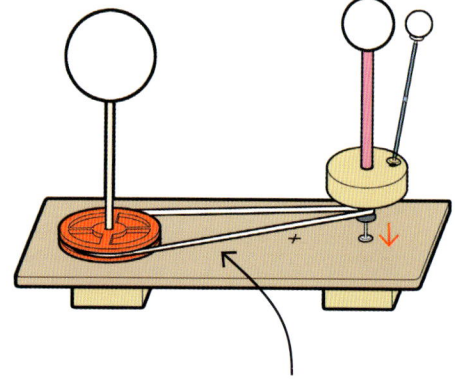

The rubber band should be slightly stretched.

 Hold the handle under the sun with one hand and rotate the base around it with the other.

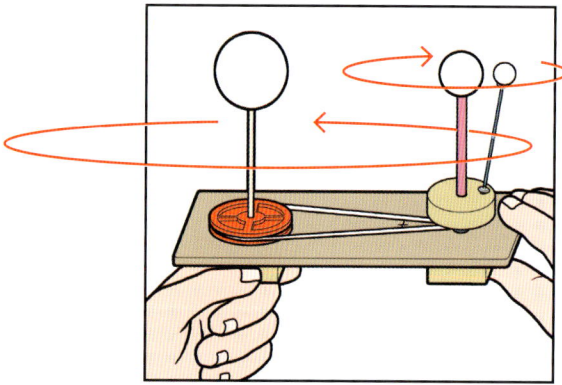

Earth should orbit the sun, the moon should orbit Earth, and Earth should spin around on its axis.

16 Paint the sun and Earth. You can also take the Earth/moon unit off and paint the base black.

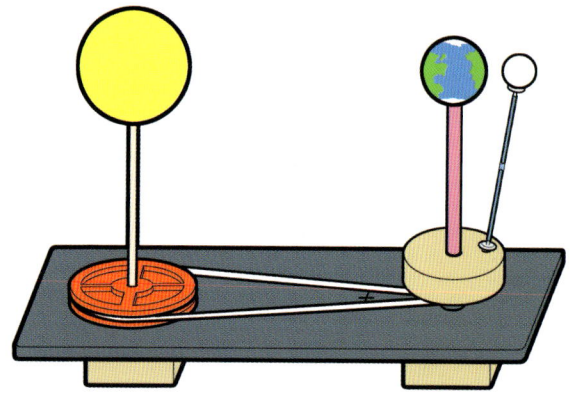

If the sun, Earth, or moon come loose, glue them back on.

NOW YOU CAN...

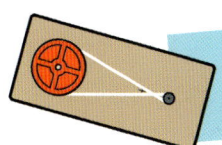

* Make the moon orbit in the correct direction around Earth by fitting the rubber band in a figure-eight shape.

* Put a flashlight next to the sun and shine it toward Earth. Can you see why, when it is daytime on one side of Earth, it is nighttime on the other side?

* Turn the motor pulley unit until the moon is between the flashlight and Earth. Look at its shadow on Earth. When the moon passes in between the sun and Earth, making a shadow, this is known as a "solar eclipse" (or eclipse of the sun).

* Turn the motor pulley unit until Earth is between the flashlight and the moon. The moon will now be in shadow. This is known as a "lunar eclipse" (or eclipse of the moon).

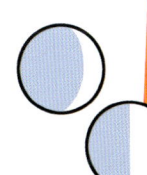

* Continue to turn the small pulley slowly and watch as the moon comes out of the shadow of Earth. Can you see why the moon appears to change shape as it orbits Earth?

HOW IT WORKS

When you hold the sun still and rotate the base around it, you are making Earth orbit the sun. In real life, this takes a year. At the same time the pulley arrangement is making the moon orbit Earth, and Earth spin around on its own axis. Half of Earth is lit up by the sun and the other half is in darkness. As Earth turns, the area where you live will go from light (daytime) to dark (nighttime) and so on.

GLOSSARY

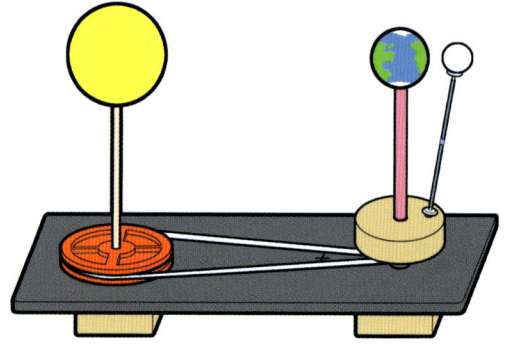

Axle A rod that passes through the center of a wheel, enabling the wheel to rotate.

Compressed air Air is a gas. The particles in a gas are quite far apart compared with a solid or a liquid, so they can be squashed together (or compressed) into a smaller space.

Force A force can be a push or a pull. You can't see it, but you can often see its effect—a force can change the speed of an object, its direction of movement, or its shape.

Friction A force between surfaces that are sliding, or trying to slide, across each other. Friction is often useful—for example, it stops bicycle tires from slipping on the road.

Gravity A force that pulls things down and makes things fall to the ground. The more mass an object has, the more force will be pulling it down.

Keel The part of a boat that sticks out from the bottom along its center line. It helps the boat to go in the direction it is pointing.

Kinetic (movement) energy The energy an object has because it is moving. The faster an object moves, and the more mass it has, the more kinetic energy it will have.

Orbit To travel in a path around another object. For example, Earth orbits the sun.

Pressure Pressure is a pushing force spread over an area. Squeezing a sealed plastic bottle puts its contents under pressure. If it is full of air, the air can be squashed easily into a smaller space, whereas water cannot.

FIND OUT MORE

For more STEM ideas and activities check out these websites:

www.exploratorium.edu/explore
www.howtosmile.org
www.lawrencehallofscience.org

WHERE TO BUY PARTS

Here are some useful suppliers of parts:

scienceprojectstore.com
allelectronics.com

LOOK OUT FOR THESE

You can find lots more exciting STEM projects for budding engineers here:

Projects
CD Racer
Teddy Bear Zip Wire
Glider
Stomp Rocket
Catapult

Projects
Coin Battery
Handheld Fan
Flashlight
Steady Hand Game
Fan Boat
Vibrating Brush Monster

Projects
Lighthouse
Traffic Lights
Chair-o-plane
Motorized Car

INDEX

axles 12, 13, 30

balloon buggy 10–13
boats 8–9, 30

Cartesian diver 6–7
colored spinner 18–21
color mixing 21
compressed air 7, 13, 30

day and night 29
Descartes, René 6

Earth 24, 26, 27, 28, 29, 30
eclipse 29
energy, kinetic 21, 30

floating 7, 9

forces 30
friction 13, 30

gravity 17, 23, 30

keel 9, 30
kinetic energy 21, 30

light 21, 29
lunar eclipse 29

marble maze 22–23
marble run 14–17
moon 24, 27, 28, 29

Newton disc 21
Newton, Sir Isaac 21

orbiting 24–29, 30

pressure 7, 30
pulleys 24, 25, 26, 27, 28, 29

rainbows 21
recycled household objects 5
rockets 13

safety 2, 5
sailboat 8–9
shadows 29
sinking 6, 7
solar eclipse 29
sun 21, 24, 25, 28, 29, 30
suppliers of parts 31

wheels 11, 12, 30

Pender County Public Library
Hampstead,
Hampstead, NC 28443

Failure to return
Library Material
is a crime —
N.C. General
Statutes # 14-398